Sedimentary ROCKS

Published in 2025 by **Cheriton Children's Books**
1 Bank Drive West, Shrewsbury, Shropshire, SY3 9DJ, UK

© Copyright 2025 Cheriton Children's Books

First Edition

Author: Sarah Eason
Designer: Paul Myerscough
Editor: Deborah Jones
Proofreader: Katie Dicker

Printed in China

Please visit our website,
www.cheritonchildrensbooks.com
to see more of our high-quality books.

CONTENTS

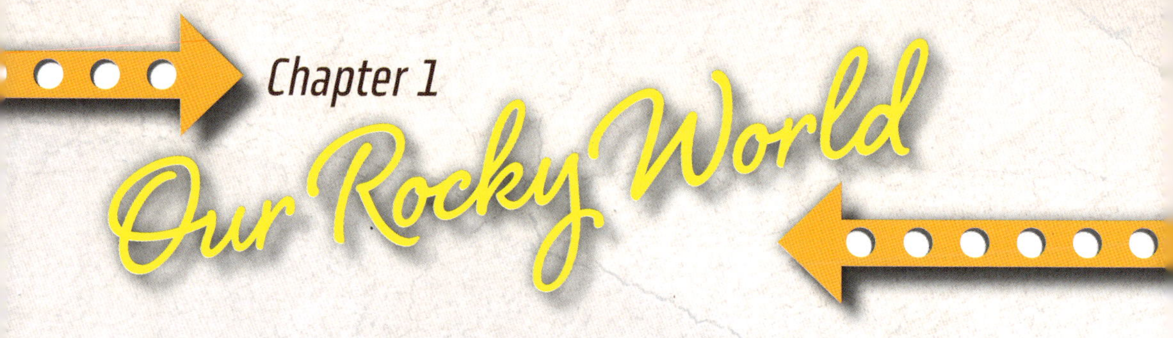

Our planet is made almost entirely of rock. It has a small metal core at its center, but the remaining 85 percent of it is rock—and that's why it is so easy to find many amazing rocks on Earth.

All Change

Although the rocky surface of our planet may seem stable, it is being reshaped and reformed all the time. Sometimes, changes to its surface can happen quickly. For example, because of a natural disaster such as a landslide or **earthquake**. Most of the time, the changes to Earth's rocky surface happen very, very slowly—so slowly that we hardly notice them. Over a very long period, surface rocks are broken down to make way for new rocks. This is part of a never-ending cycle called the rock cycle.

Sedimentary rock can begin as pieces of other rocks that have been worn away over many years.

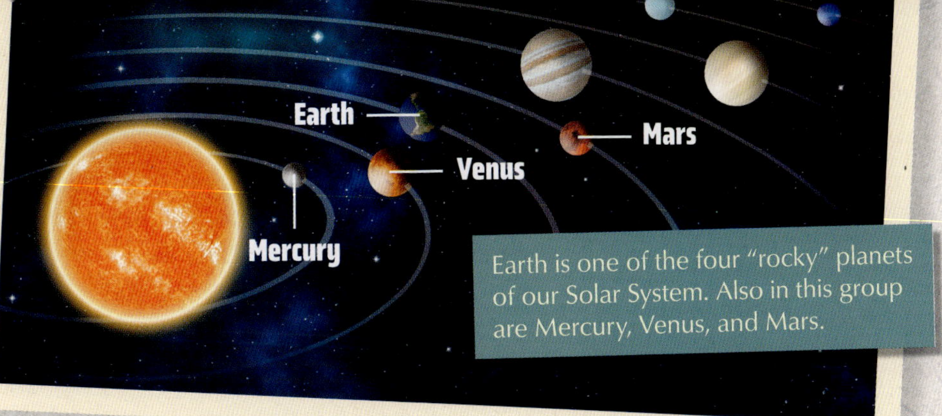

Earth's Rock Cycle

The rock cycle is a process by which one type of rock changes into another type of rock. Earth has three main types of rock: igneous rock, metamorphic rock, and sedimentary rock. Each can change into another type when affected by temperature, **weathering**, and **pressure**.

How Rock Changes

When heated deep underground, rocks turn into liquid rock. We call this melted rock magma. When rocks are worn away by weathering or erosion, they break into smaller pieces called **sediment**. Rock can also be squeezed under great pressure, which also forces it to change.

Understanding Rock Types

Igneous rock is magma that has cooled and hardened. This can happen above or below the ground. Igneous rock changes by melting into magma, eroding into sediment, or being pressed so tightly that it becomes metamorphic rock.

Metamorphic rock began life as igneous or sedimentary rock that was then heated and squeezed. Metamorphic rock can change again by eroding into sediment or melting into magma.

Sedimentary rock is made up of squashed sediments from other rocks, plus the remains of living things. It can erode back into sediment, be squeezed into metamorphic rock, or melted into magma.

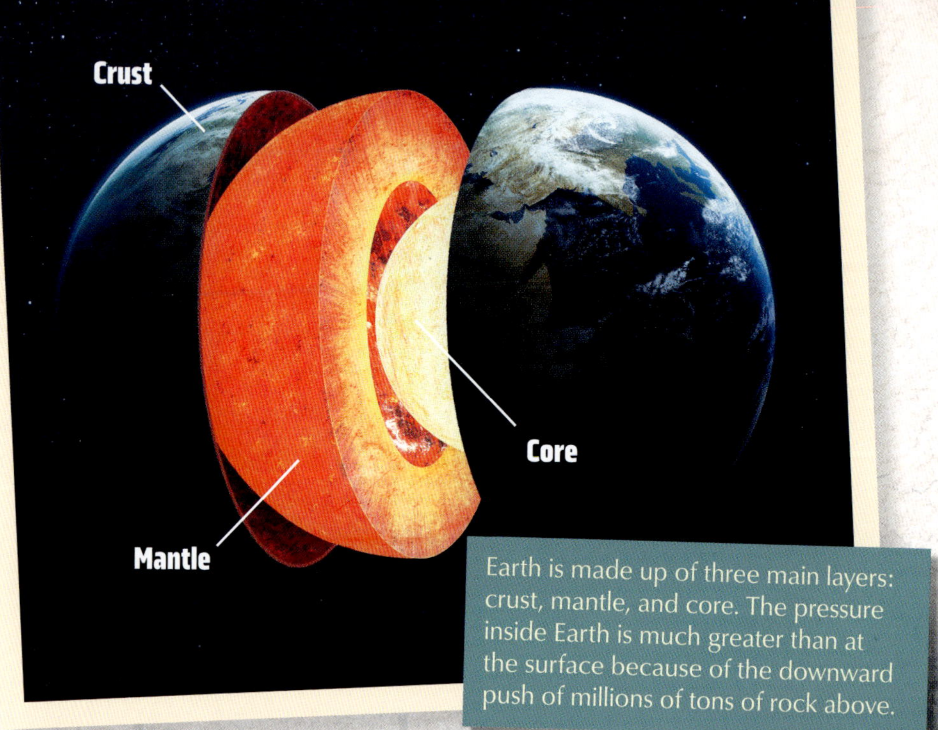

Earth is made up of three main layers: crust, mantle, and core. The pressure inside Earth is much greater than at the surface because of the downward push of millions of tons of rock above.

Look Inside Earth

To understand the rock cycle and why rock is so affected by temperature, weathering, and pressure, we need to first look at the structure of Earth.

Earth looks solid and immovable at the surface, but inside are layers that are not at all like the surface. In fact, Earth is made up of three very different parts.

Crust: This is the outer part of our planet. It is the section on which we live. It is up to 44 miles (70 km) thick and is broken up into enormous parts, called plates.

Mantle: This mostly solid layer moves around and is about 1,800 miles (2,900 km) thick. Earth's plates float on the mantle.

Core: This is the hottest part of our planet and it forms the center of Earth. The center of the core reaches nearly 12,000 degrees Fahrenheit (6,700 °C), hot enough to keep it permanently molten, or liquid.

Rock Recycling

During the rock cycle, new rock material can rise to the surface from deep within Earth. But most surface rocks are made from existing rock that is continually recycled. For example, as a rock is weathered, a grain within it may be loosened. That grain may then become part of another rock. It will then be weathered and separated from that rock, and form part of a new rock, repeatedly.

Take a Rock Cycle Road Trip!

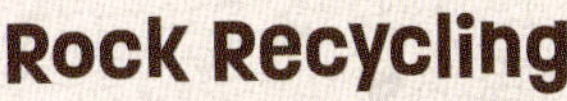

In this book, we will explore how sedimentary rock is created, where we can find it, and why it is so useful to us. We'll take an amazing rock cycle road trip to discover the rock cycle in action, some of the most spectacular sedimentary rock sites in the world, incredible sedimentary rocks, and the amazing and famous things that are made from them. So, what are you waiting for? Let's hit the road and discover a world that rocks!

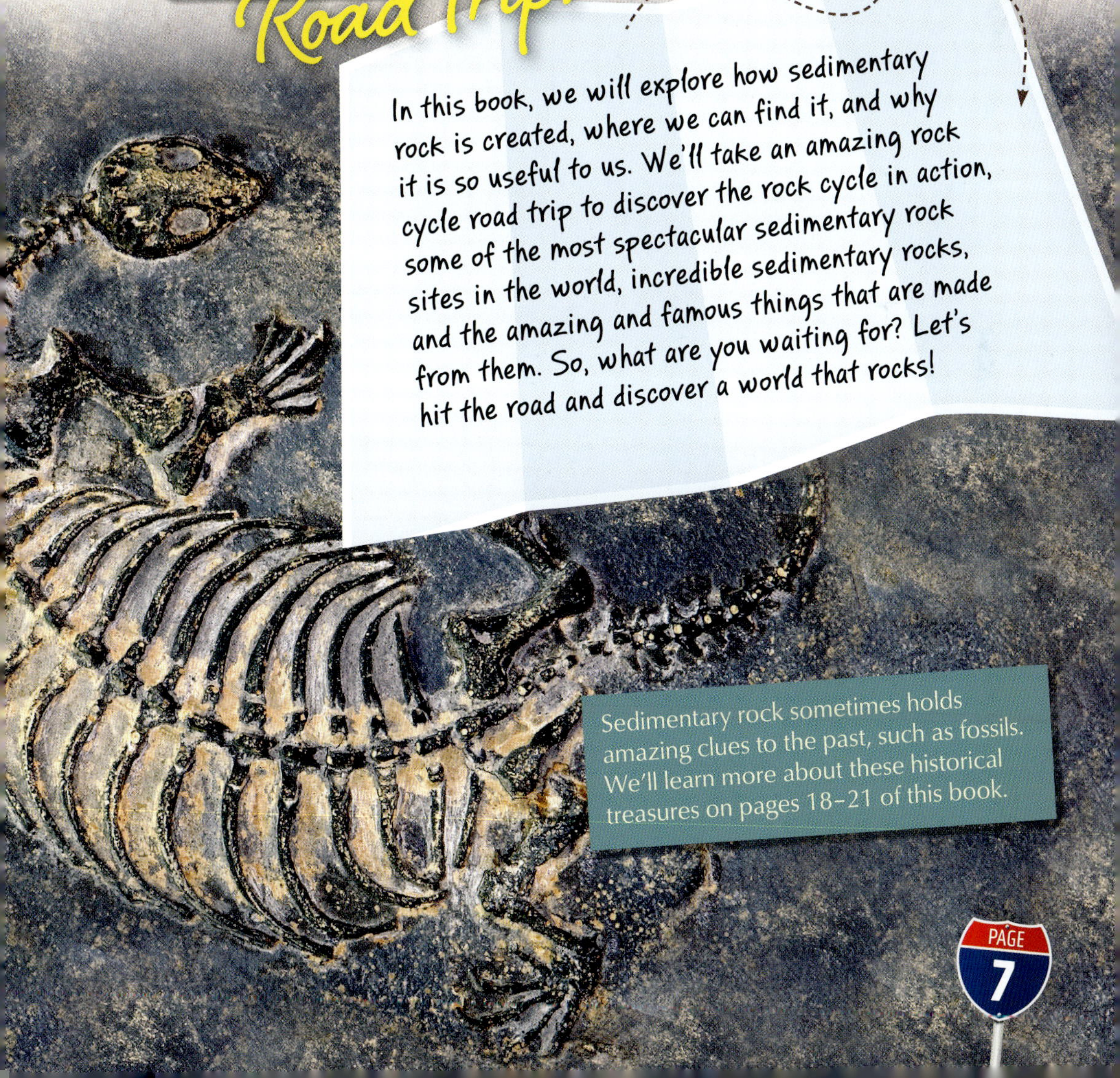

Sedimentary rock sometimes holds amazing clues to the past, such as fossils. We'll learn more about these historical treasures on pages 18–21 of this book.

Sedimentary rock has many layers and is usually softer than igneous or metamorphic rock. It is made from layers of sediment that have become hard. About three-quarters of Earth's land surface and most of the ocean floor is covered by sedimentary rock. The rocks differ depending on the types of sediments they contain. For example, sandstone is rock made from billions of sand grains.

Weighed Down with Pressure

One layer of rock sediment weighs many tons but imagine the weight of tens or hundreds of layers! Under the enormous weight of the rock layers above, the lower layers of sediment are pressed so hard that all the water in the layers is pushed out. Some **minerals** present in the sediments **dissolve** in the water and glue the sediment grains together. This is how sedimentary rock forms. Over many years, as more layers of sediment form on Earth's surface, more rock is formed in the squashed layers of sediment beneath.

Grains of sand were once rock that was broken down into very tiny pieces. Over thousands of years, the grains can be pressed together to form rock once more.

Not all sediments are pieces of worn-down rock. Some are parts of shells from dead ocean animals. Others are tiny grains of light ash from volcanic **eruptions**.

Piled High and Heated

Sedimentary rocks start to form whenever debris, such as sand, mud, and **organic remains**, begins to settle on the beds of seas and lakes, or is piled up by the wind and rivers. As these sediments settle, they are buried and compacted, or pressed together, by the weight of sediments above. Over thousands or millions of years, the pressure, combined with the warmth inside Earth, turns the sediments into layers of solid rock.

The Sedimentary Stars

There are many sedimentary rocks on Earth. Some of the best known are rock salt, sandstone, chalk, shale, limestone.

Digging Deeper

All rocks are made from one or more minerals. In a rock, the minerals are solid. However, in magma, they have melted and bonded together. When magma cools, the different minerals in it each start to form solid, regular-shaped **crystals** that we call grains when identifying rocks.

Crumbling Mountains

Rock is hard and heavy. However, did you know that water can cause entire mountains of rock to move and crumble into pieces? When water fills a crack during winter, it sometimes freezes into ice in the cold air. Ice takes up more space than water and forces the crack to widen a little. Imagine this process happening thousands of times, over thousands of years. This is one example of weathering.

From Rock to Grain

Huge rocks are reduced to tiny grains during weathering. Rocks also undergo weathering when plant roots grow into them or when wind blows sand against the rock, scratching its surface.

The Ganges River crumbles rock as it flows from its mountain source, carrying the worn-away sediment in its water.

Digging Deeper

The salt we put on our food is halite, or rock salt, that has been ground into tiny pieces! It formed when water in ancient seas **evaporated**. During evaporation, the minerals that had dissolved in the water turned into solid salt crystals.

Carried Away

Rushing water in a river, heavy rainfall, pounding waves on a beach, or gusts of strong wind can all carry rock grains from one place to another. These are examples of weathering and erosion. When water or wind slows down, the grains of rock they carry fall to the ground or sink underwater.

The Ganges and Brahmaputra Rivers in southern Asia erode more sediment than any other river. Head this way to check out these sediment-carrying wonders!

ROCK STOP! **GANGES AND BRAHMAPUTRA RIVERS, ASIA**

The Ganges and Brahmaputra Rivers form one of the largest river systems in the world, flowing from the Himalaya Mountains in Asia through India, eventually emptying into the Bay of Bengal. As the rivers flow, the water washes away sediment. Some of this is rock weathered from the Himalaya Mountains as the rivers flow through them. The sediment is washed into the rivers by streams and rainwater. Each year, the rivers move more than 1.1 billion tons (1 billion mt) of sediment. This is enough to fill about half the cargo ships on Earth!

The sediment carried by the Ganges River is rich in **nutrients**. As it flows, the river **deposits** sediment along its shores. The sediment improves the quality of the soil there, creating **fertile** areas of farmland that people have relied on for centuries.

ROCK SALT
What a Rock Star!

Halite is the mineral name for salt. A rock made up mostly of halite is a sedimentary rock known as rock salt. Rock salt forms where large amounts of inland sea water or salty lake water evaporate, leaving the salt in the water behind.

Rock Star Characteristics

- Usually white but can be different colors, such as yellow, green, black, brown, and red if **impurities** come into contact with the rock
- Relatively soft and can be easily scratched
- Salty to the taste

Himalayan rock salt is probably the best-known rock salt in the world. It is **mined** in the Khewra Salt Mine of the southern Himalayas, in Pakistan, Asia. Himalayan salt is often pink because it contains small amounts of **iron oxide**.

Rock Cycle
Road Trip!

Rock Salt Hotspots

Rock salt is found all over the world in places where seas and salty lakes have evaporated. The following countries are the biggest producers of rock salt:

THAT ROCKS!

The Khewra Salt Mine was discovered around 320 BCE when the famous Greek leader Alexander the Great traveled through the area that is today Pakistan.

Many Years in the Making

Conglomerates are coarse-grained sedimentary rocks. They formed over thousands of years as sediments were deposited. Conglomerates are made from large pieces of rounded gravel or pebbles.

A Moving Story

The edges of the pebbles were rounded when they were picked up by moving water and tossed against other pebbles and rocks. The pebbles or gravel were then dropped onto beaches or in river channels, where they built up into piles of sediment. Over time, the weight of these piles squashed the tiny pieces of sand and clay, and the water, between the pebbles. This formed a substance a little like cement, which stuck the pebbles together.

Rough and Tumble

For a conglomerate to form, large pieces of sediment must exist upstream in a body of water such as a river, lake, or ocean. The sediments are rolled and tumbled by moving waters such as a gushing stream or the waves of the ocean, often across long distances.

The many smaller rocks that this conglomerate was formed from can be clearly seen.

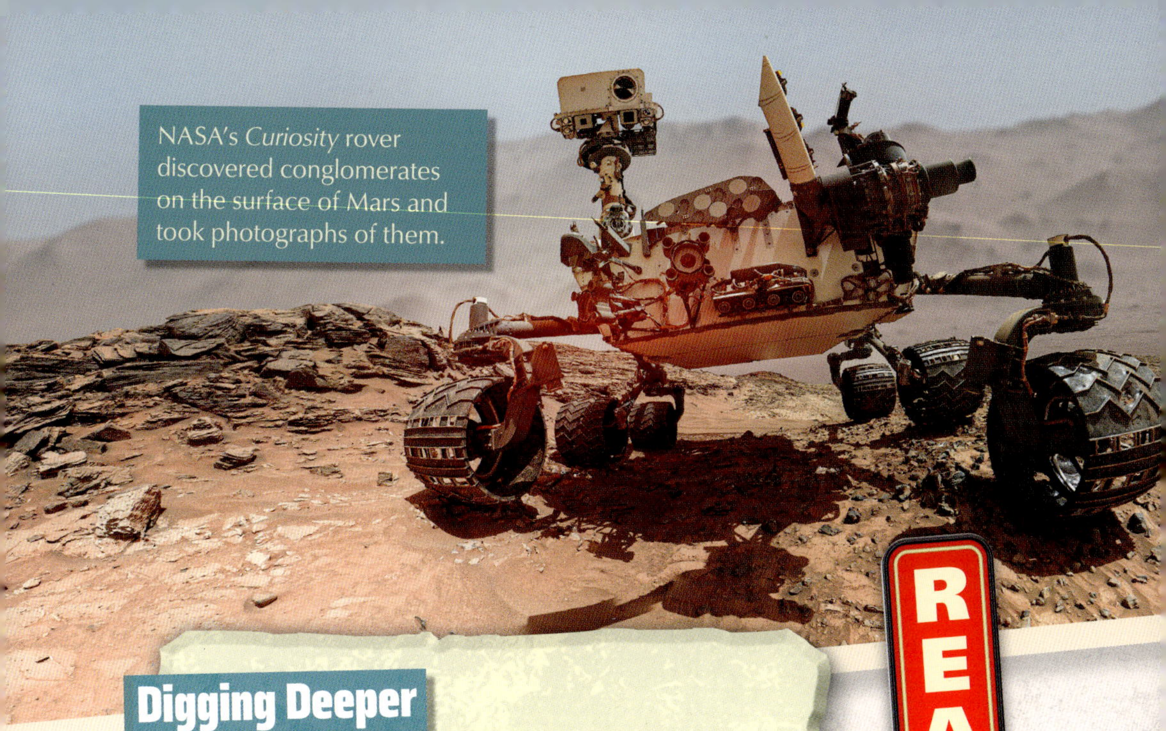

NASA's *Curiosity* rover discovered conglomerates on the surface of Mars and took photographs of them.

Digging Deeper

Some conglomerate rock has been found on the surface of the planet Mars. The rounded gravel in the conglomerate is evidence that a stream or a beach had moved the rocks and shaped them into rounded pebbles. This proves that water once flowed on Mars!

Only a Few Uses

Conglomerates do not break cleanly, and because they are made up of different sizes and types of rocks it is difficult to know how strong they are until they are tested. This makes them difficult to use. Conglomerates that are only weakly cemented together can be crushed to make **aggregate** for concrete.

Diamond Finder

Certain rocks in conglomerates can be used to find diamonds! Most diamonds are found in an igneous rock called kimberlite. If a conglomerate contains lumps of kimberlite, it tells people that there may be some kimberlite containing diamonds somewhere upstream.

The photo's caption box:

Some amazing examples of sedimentary strata can be seen at The Wave in Arizona.

Layer Upon Layer

Over millions of years, layers of sediment pile up on each other and turn into layers of sedimentary rock, called strata. In any area of sedimentary rock, the oldest sediment layers were deposited first. They are found at the bottom of the rock. Moving up the rock, the layers become younger and younger. The layer at the surface is the youngest of all. Sedimentary rocks can be different depths, but the deepest can be more than 9 miles (15 km) deep!

Shaping Strata

In some places, sedimentary rock has vertical or wavy layers. However, it did not always look like this. Over time, movements in the enormous blocks of rock under Earth's surface pushed the horizontal strata of sedimentary rock upward. The rock at the surface also became weathered and eroded. Some of the rock grains even became part of new sedimentary rocks!

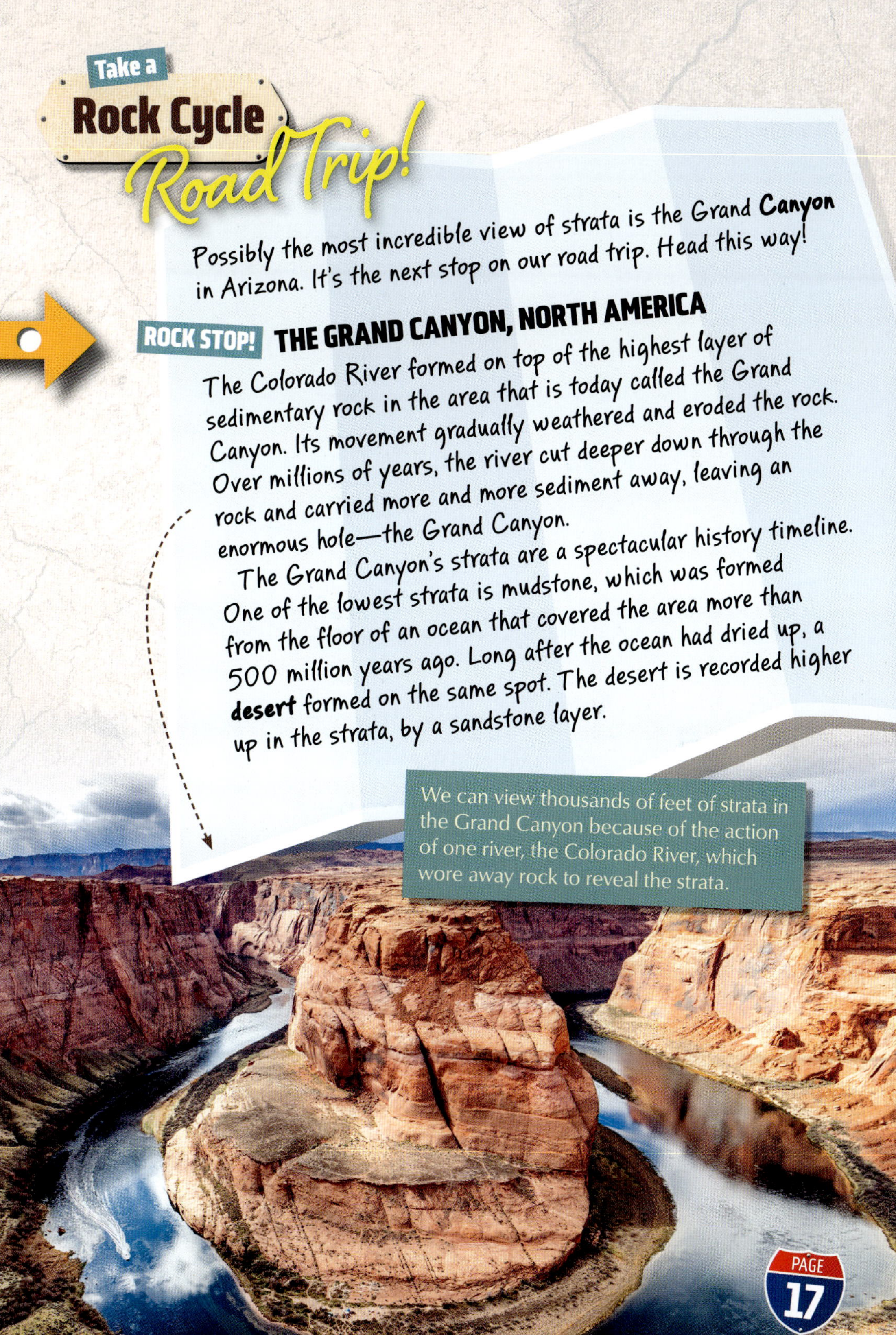

Possibly the most incredible view of strata is the Grand **Canyon** in Arizona. It's the next stop on our road trip. Head this way!

ROCK STOP! ### THE GRAND CANYON, NORTH AMERICA

The Colorado River formed on top of the highest layer of sedimentary rock in the area that is today called the Grand Canyon. Its movement gradually weathered and eroded the rock. Over millions of years, the river cut deeper down through the rock and carried more and more sediment away, leaving an enormous hole—the Grand Canyon.

The Grand Canyon's strata are a spectacular history timeline. One of the lowest strata is mudstone, which was formed from the floor of an ocean that covered the area more than 500 million years ago. Long after the ocean had dried up, a **desert** formed on the same spot. The desert is recorded higher up in the strata, by a sandstone layer.

We can view thousands of feet of strata in the Grand Canyon because of the action of one river, the Colorado River, which wore away rock to reveal the strata.

Fossil Finds

Imagine that you are
walking on a beach and
you spot some sedimentary
rock with a strange, shell-
shaped pattern. It looks
a little like the shells you
might find in a rock pool. You
have found a fossil! A fossil
is all that is left of something
that lived long, long ago.

Making a Fossil

Fossils are the remains of living
things that are preserved, or kept from rotting,
in rock. Fossils form over millions of years after
dead plants or animals become covered with
layer upon layer of sediment. The soft parts
of the plants and animals mostly rot away.
However, the tough, hard parts last longer.
Minerals in the sediment soak through the
hard remains and turn them into stone.

Leaving Only a Trace

Some ancient living things did not become
complete fossils, but still left traces of their
lives in the rocks. These are called trace fossils.
They include the tracks left by animals as they
walked or ran along the ground. Pieces of feathers
or hair that fell from animals as they moved, or
leaves that fell from trees and bushes, can all
form trace fossils. Even animal droppings and
other waste can fossilize. Trace fossils tell us how
animals and plants of the distant past lived.

Trace fossil finds, like this dinosaur's footprint, make exciting discoveries.

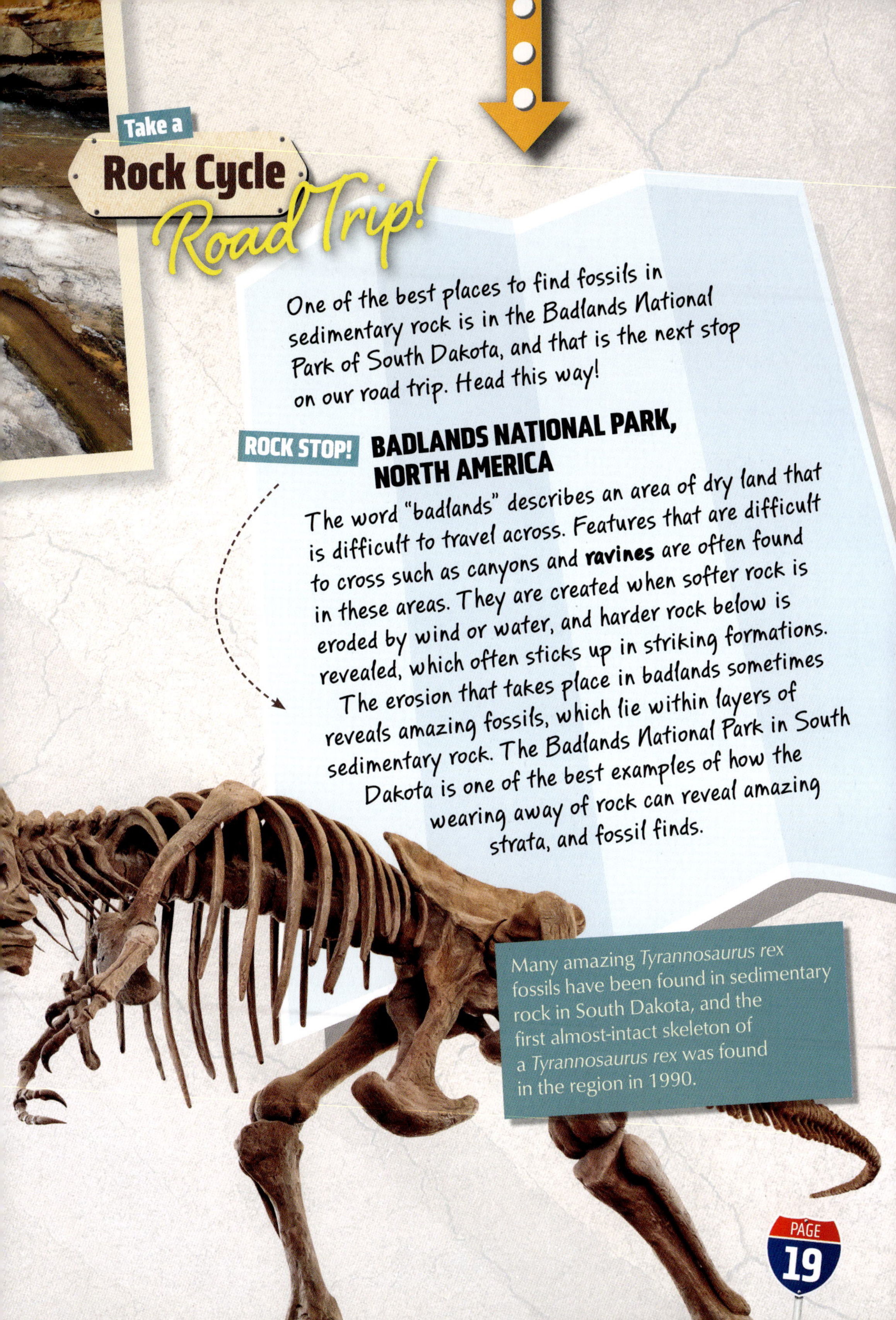

One of the best places to find fossils in sedimentary rock is in the Badlands National Park of South Dakota, and that is the next stop on our road trip. Head this way!

ROCK STOP! BADLANDS NATIONAL PARK, NORTH AMERICA

The word "badlands" describes an area of dry land that is difficult to travel across. Features that are difficult to cross such as canyons and **ravines** are often found in these areas. They are created when softer rock is eroded by wind or water, and harder rock below is revealed, which often sticks up in striking formations.

The erosion that takes place in badlands sometimes reveals amazing fossils, which lie within layers of sedimentary rock. The Badlands National Park in South Dakota is one of the best examples of how the wearing away of rock can reveal amazing strata, and fossil finds.

Many amazing *Tyrannosaurus rex* fossils have been found in sedimentary rock in South Dakota, and the first almost-intact skeleton of a *Tyrannosaurus rex* was found in the region in 1990.

FOSSILS

What a Rock Star!

One of the most amazing things about sedimentary rocks is that they contain many fossils, which are preserved in the rock. Fossils are like windows to the past, because they tell us about the time and place that a rock formed.

Rock Star Characteristics

- Most fossils are found in earth that was once underwater
- Fossils are typically found in sedimentary rock rather than igneous or metamorphic rock

Badlands landscapes, like the one in South Dakota, have an otherworldly appearance because of their dramatic rock formations.

THAT ROCKS!

Some fossils are **imprints** on soft material that later became hard rock. They include trace fossils.

Sometimes, fossils are created when a small insect or a piece of a plant, such as a leaf, becomes trapped in a sticky substance called resin. When the resin hardens, it changes into a rocklike material called amber. The object trapped in the resin is then preserved inside the amber.

Take a
Rock Cycle
Road Trip!

Fossil Hotspots

Other great dinosaur fossil finds have taken place all over the world, but the greatest variety of **species** have been found in these areas:

Chapter 3

Sedimentary Stars

Sedimentary rocks cover much of our planet's surface, and they are being constantly reshaped. This sedimentary surface has an enormous effect on Earth, influencing everything from the way life on our planet evolves, to the formation of huge mountain ranges. Let's look at some of the rocks that are sedimentary superstars.

Stone Made from Sand

Sandstone is formed from sand, which is made up of small grains of rock that were eroded from larger rocks. Sandstone is easy to cut and carve, but unlike limestone, it is resistant to weathering. For this reason, it is often used for building and to make pavers. Most sandstone contains quartz grains. Quartz is a common mineral. It is also very hard and tough, so is difficult to wear down. Sandstone formed from quartz grains alone is known as quartzite and is very hard.

Digging Deeper

Fossils are often found in sandstone, providing clues about creatures that once lived in ancient waters. However, sandstone also reveals other things about ancient seas and oceans. Have you seen sand on a beach piled up in ripples or carved into curved lines by the waves? Sometimes, sand becomes buried and hardens into rock, with the ripple marks still visible. This reveals the movements of water millions of years ago.

One of the most famous examples of sandstone is Table Mountain in South Africa. It's the next stop on our road trip. Head this way!

ROCK STOP! ### TABLE MOUNTAIN, AFRICA

The Table Mountain Sandstone (TMS) is a group of rock formations in a mountain belt in South Africa called the Cape Supergroup. They are made up of sandstone and were created between 510 and 340 million years ago. TMS is made up of the hardest rock in the Cape Supergroup and has withstood weathering and erosion for millions of years, which is why today its mountains form the highest peaks in the area.

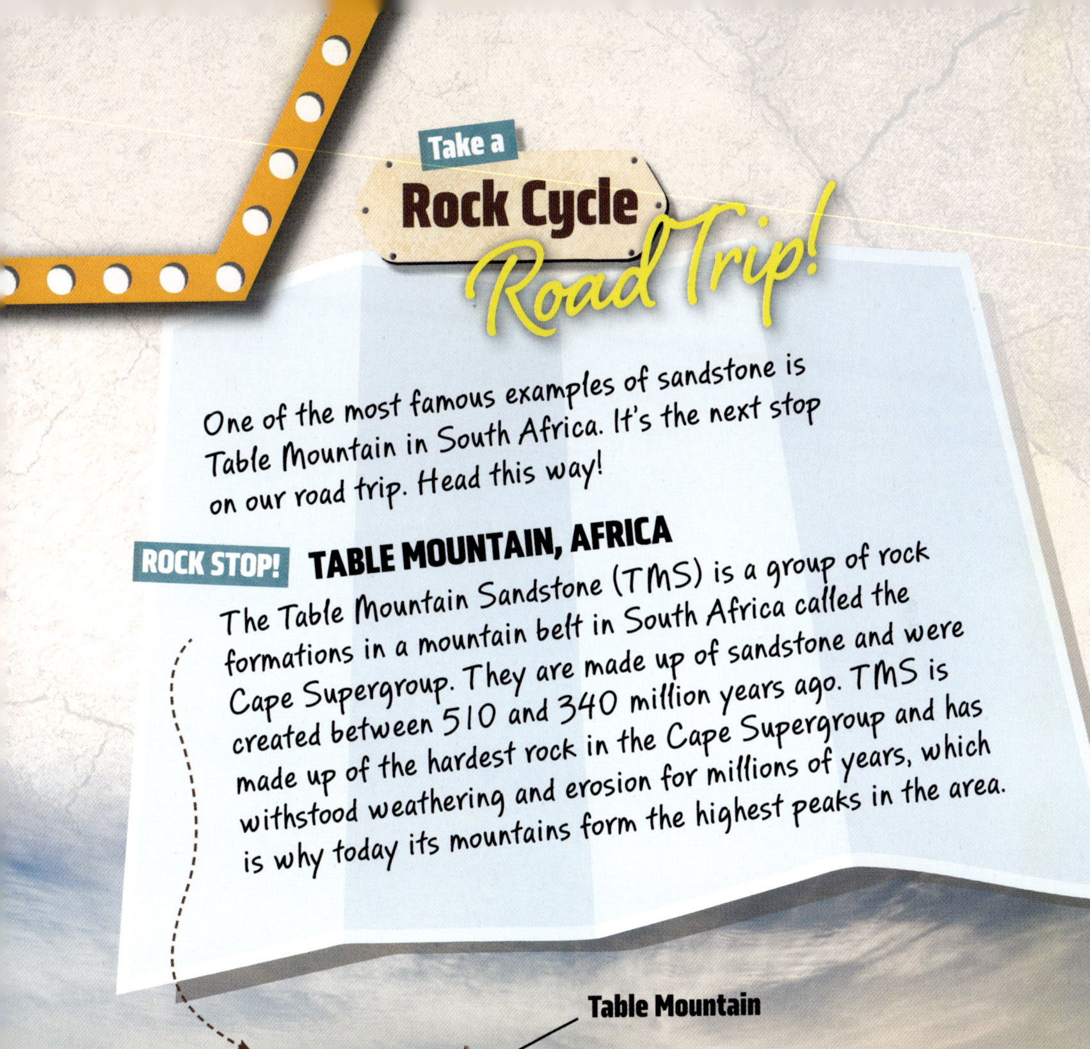

Table Mountain is the most famous peak of the TMS group and rises behind the city of Cape Town in South Africa.

SANDSTONE
What a Rock Star!

Sandstone contains tiny pieces of rock, minerals, or **organic material**. These pieces were reduced to tiny grains of sand over many years of weathering. The tiny pieces of sand were then carried away by water, wind, or ice. Once deposited, the grains were pressed tightly together over thousands or millions of years. The joined grains then formed sandstone rock.

Rock Star Characteristics

- Porous, which means the rock has many tiny holes into which water can easily move
- Often yellow-brown in color but can also range in color from tan and gray to white and pink
- Rough and gritty to the touch

Sandstone is one of the most common types of sedimentary rock and is found around the world. The Externsteine is a famous sandstone rock formation in Germany, Europe.

Rock Cycle
Road Trip!

Sandstone Hotspots
Places where a lot of sandstone is found include:

Did YOU Know?

We can learn a lot about the past by studying sandstone. For example, if the grains in sandstone are very rounded, it tells us that they were transported over a long distance. If the surface of the rock is frosty in appearance, that is usually a sign that the sand was transported by wind from a sandy desert area.

THAT ROCKS!

Sandstone is the official state rock of Nevada. Amazing sandstone formations can be seen in the state at the Valley of Fire State Park.

Ancient Mud

Mudstone is made from ancient mud. The very tiny grains of clay inside this rock are so small that they can only be seen with a magnifying glass. Clay is a type of fine-grained soil or mud.

Making Mudstone

Mudstone forms when tiny pieces of clay settle on the bottom of oceans, lakes, or even calm riverbeds. Over time, the mud is buried by heavy layers of sediment, which squeeze the water out of the mud and turn it into mudstone. Sometimes, mud, silt, and clay are compressed, or squashed, into a soft, dark-colored mudstone called shale.

Many Uses

High-quality clays or mudstones are used to make pottery. Bricks and roof tiles are often made from mudstone. Cement is made from crushed mudstone that has been heated and mixed with limestone. Shale also splits very easily into thin sheets, so it is used to make floor and roof tiles.

Releasing Oil

Oil shale contains substances that can be used to make oil. However, oil from shale is expensive to buy because a lot of energy is needed to extract, or take out, the oil. The rock must be heated to temperatures reaching 932 degrees Fahrenheit (500 °C) to release the oil, then the rock is cooled.

The Burgess Shale is found in the Rocky Mountains in British Columbia, Canada. It is famous because it contains some amazingly ancient fossils. Head this way!

ROCK STOP! ## THE BURGESS SHALE, NORTH AMERICA

The Burgess Shale is a world-famous fossil field that was discovered in the Canadian Rocky Mountains in 1909. The shale here is special because its strata contain tens of thousands of rare fossils.

The fossils include many delicate, soft-bodied creatures that date from around 500 million years ago. Before 1909, the remains of such creatures had never been found. Many had very unusual features and were quite unlike any other known animals. Some had five eyes and a nose like the hose of a vacuum cleaner!

This trilobite fossil was found in the Burgess Shale. It is more than 270 million years old!

SHALE
What a Rock Star!

Shale is the most abundant sedimentary rock on Earth and is found all over the planet. About 70 percent of all sedimentary rock is shale.

Rock Star Characteristics

- Breaks into long, thin pieces with sharp edges
- Can be black, gray, red, brown, or yellow
- Much of the world's oil and natural gas is found in areas of shale rock

THAT ROCKS!

Shale has not been found on Earth alone. The Mars rovers have found areas of shale rock on Mars, which look just like the shale found on Earth.

A lot of shale rock is found in Canada.

Rock Cycle
Road Trip!

Shale Hotspots

Places where a lot of shale is found include:

Did You Know?

Oil and natural gas are mined in large areas of shale rock. The fuel is often obtained by drilling into the rock and using high temperatures to extract the oil and gas. A lot of oil and gas is very difficult to remove from the rock because it is trapped in tiny spaces within it.

Made from Tiny Animals

Limestone rock is formed from the remains of billions of tiny sea creatures. As the creatures died, their bodies built up on the ocean floor, eventually turning into limestone. This rock can be used for many different things and it is an important **resource**.

Fossils found in the Monument Rocks area (see opposite) include giant swimming reptiles, 20-feet- (6 m) long fish, and enormous clams up to 6 feet (1.8 m) in diameter.

Shells and Skeletons

Limestone is mostly formed from the mineral calcite, which is a type of **calcium carbonate**. Sea animals, such as oysters and **coral**, take in calcite from seawater. Calcite forms bones and shells. When the animals die, the soft parts of their bodies rot away. Their skeletons and shells, which contain calcite, sink to the ocean floor. There, they later turn into limestone.

Built for Building

Limestone is an important stone used for buildings and statues. The only problem with limestone is that **acids** in rainwater can slowly weather and erode its surface. Limestone is heated to make lime, which is used to create the two most important building materials on Earth: concrete and steel.

Digging Deeper

Chalk is a soft, pale type of very fine-grained limestone. It crumbles easily to a fine powder. In the past, people used chalk lumps to write on slates and ground-up chalk to clean their teeth. Even today, some toothpaste contains chalk.

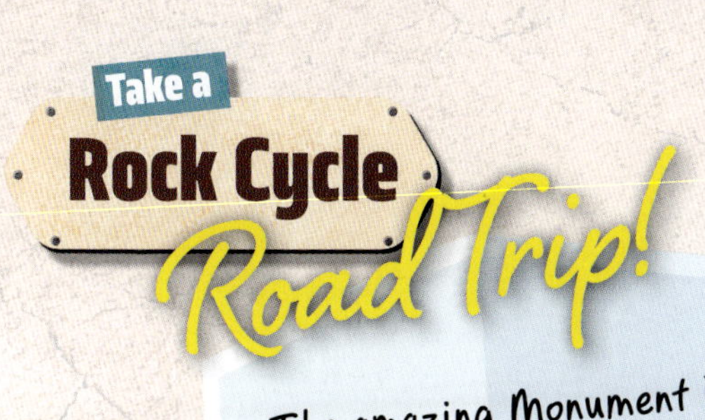

The amazing Monument Rocks National Landmark in Kansas are also known as the Chalk Pyramids. Let's take a look!

ROCK STOP!

MONUMENT ROCKS, NORTH AMERICA

The towering formations can be as tall as 70 feet (21 m) and include amazing features such as **buttes** and arches. They are mainly made of chalk and were formed from sediment that was deposited in the area over millions of years. Erosion thinned areas of rock over many years, with only the harder, tougher areas remaining to form the incredible towering formations that can be seen today.

Many fossils of creatures with calcium-filled shells have been found in the Monument Rocks area. The fossils show that 80 million years ago, the region was covered by an ocean that was full of tiny, shelled animals.

Towering limestone rock formations, with arches cut into their centers, are some of the amazing features of Monument Rocks.

CHALK
What a Rock Star!

Chalk forms from a very fine-grained ocean sediment called ooze. It is created when ocean creatures die and their remains sink to the seabed. There, they gather and form the slimy and mushy substance that is ooze.

Rock Star Characteristics

- Very soft and easy to break
- Usually white or light gray in color
- Extremely porous

Chalk is widely found in western Europe, where it can often be seen as a bright rock in vertical cliffs along shorelines. The White Cliffs of Dover, England, are a famous chalk landmark.

Chalk Hotspots

A lot of chalk is found in the United States, particularly in these states:

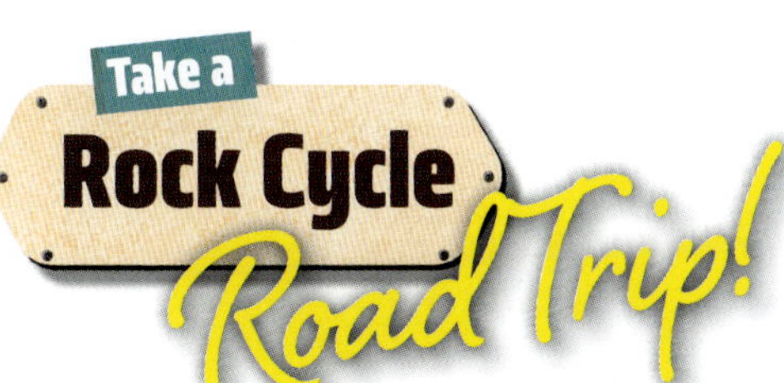

THAT ROCKS!

A great deal of chalk was deposited during the Cretaceous Period around 145 to 66 million years ago, when dinosaurs roamed Earth. During that time, warm seas were found in many parts of the world, in which a lot of bony and shelled sea creatures lived. When they died, the calcium carbonate in their shells and skeletons easily broke down in the warm water. That resulted in the production of a lot of ooze from which chalk formed.

Underground World

Limestone is a sedimentary rock that can be dissolved and worn away by rainwater. This creates caves below Earth's surface. In these underground worlds, rock takes on awesome new forms!

More than 119 caves made up the amazing Carlsbad Caverns National Park (see opposite).

Carving Out Caves

Caves form gradually in underground layers of limestone rock. Rainwater seeps into the ground through cracks in the surface and by soaking into underground rocks. Over time, rainwater dissolves more and more limestone, causing small gaps to widen into big caves. As rainwater weakens layers of limestone, large chunks of it may fall from cave ceilings, making the caves even bigger.

Rock Icicles

Limestone caves are not simply empty holes. Incredible, icicle-shaped rocks hang from cave ceilings and rise from cave floors. These are stalactites and stalagmites. A stalactite is made when mineral-rich water drips from a cave ceiling. A stalagmite is made when mineral-rich water drips onto the cave floor and builds up into a structure. Sometimes, stalactites and stalagmites grow together to form a pillar that stretches from the ceiling of the cave to its floor.

Digging Deeper

Stalactites start out as narrow mineral tubes that hang down from cave ceilings. They grow thicker and wider as water trickles down them, depositing more mineral layers on top of the early layers. Scientists can tell how old stalactites are by their width. When a stalactite breaks off, rings inside show the growth history of the stalactite.

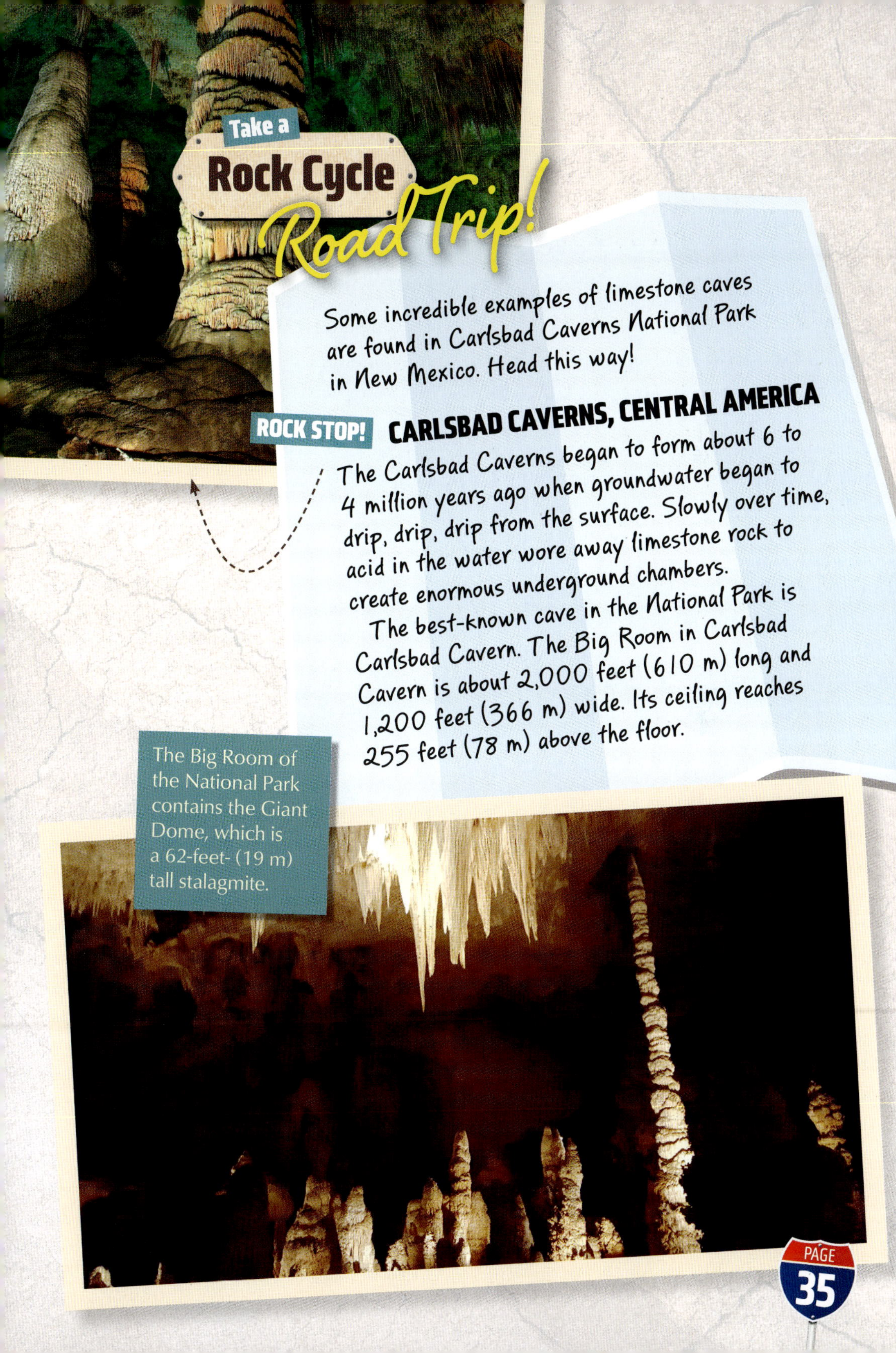

Some incredible examples of limestone caves are found in Carlsbad Caverns National Park in New Mexico. Head this way!

ROCK STOP! CARLSBAD CAVERNS, CENTRAL AMERICA

The Carlsbad Caverns began to form about 6 to 4 million years ago when groundwater began to drip, drip, drip from the surface. Slowly over time, acid in the water wore away limestone rock to create enormous underground chambers.

The best-known cave in the National Park is Carlsbad Cavern. The Big Room in Carlsbad Cavern is about 2,000 feet (610 m) long and 1,200 feet (366 m) wide. Its ceiling reaches 255 feet (78 m) above the floor.

The Big Room of the National Park contains the Giant Dome, which is a 62-feet- (19 m) tall stalagmite.

LIMESTONE
What a Rock Star!

Limestone usually forms in very clear, calm, warm, and shallow ocean and sea waters. That is because limestone is largely made up of calcium carbonate, which is found in the remains of shelled and bony sea creatures. When they die, their shells and skeletons break down on the seabed. Limestone forms from these remains.

Rock Star Characteristics

- Very soft and easy to break
- Usually white or light gray in color
- Extremely porous

Today, limestone is forming in the warm waters of the Caribbean Sea, where beautiful, shelled creatures such as sea turtles swim.

Limestone Hotspots

Limestone is also forming in these warm waters:

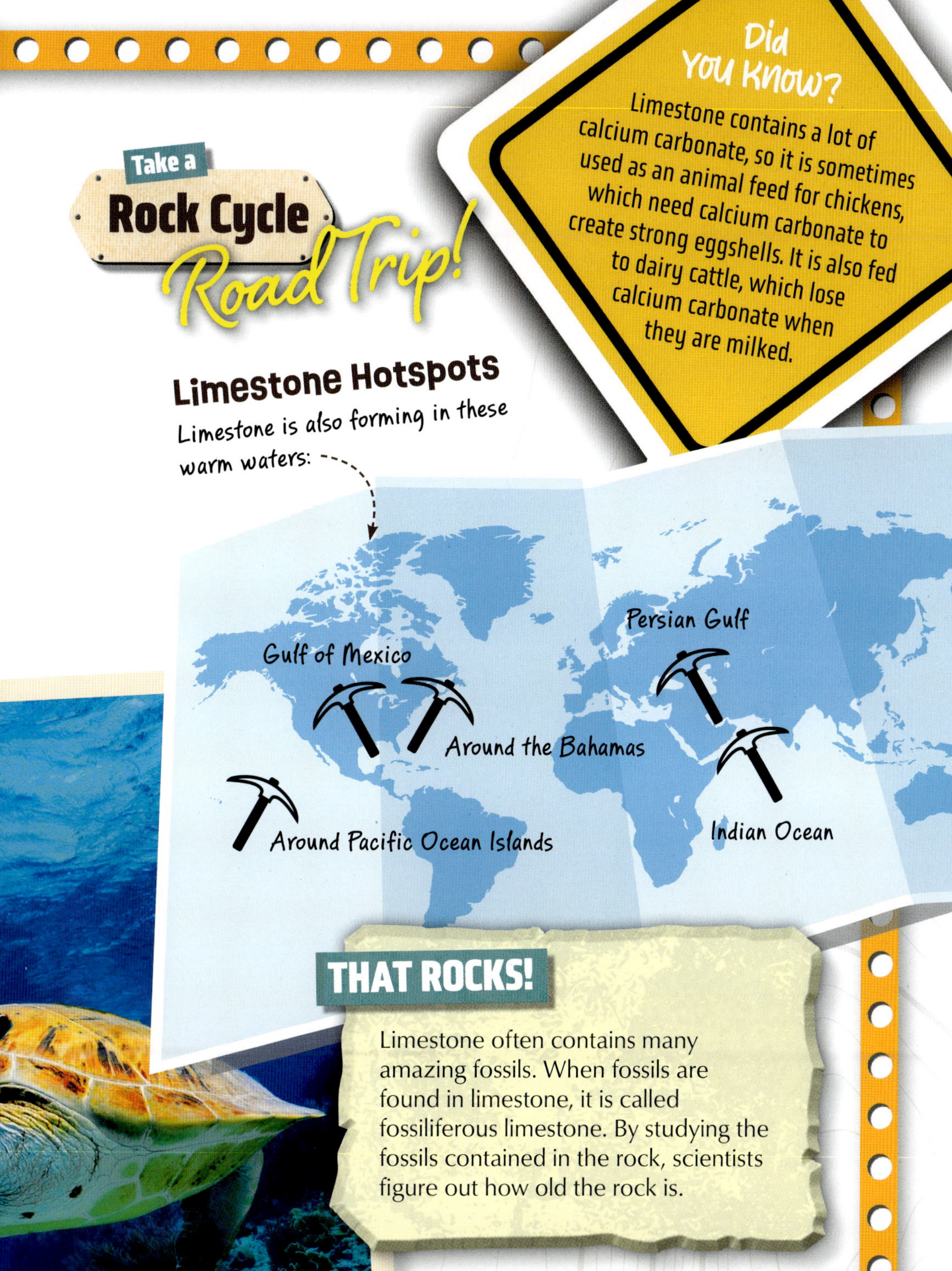

THAT ROCKS!

Limestone often contains many amazing fossils. When fossils are found in limestone, it is called fossiliferous limestone. By studying the fossils contained in the rock, scientists figure out how old the rock is.

The Power of Sedimentary Rock

People get most of the energy needed to power machines from fossil fuels. These include coal, gas, and oil. These fossil fuels are always found between sedimentary rock strata.

Powered by Sedimentary

Coal is a hard rock formed from ancient forests that have been buried and squashed by sediment. It is widely used as a fuel in power stations that produce the electricity we need to power our computers and light our homes. Gas and oil are mostly formed from the remains of ocean plankton that were trapped among strata. Gas is used in power stations but also to heat homes. Oil is made into diesel and other fuels that power vehicles.

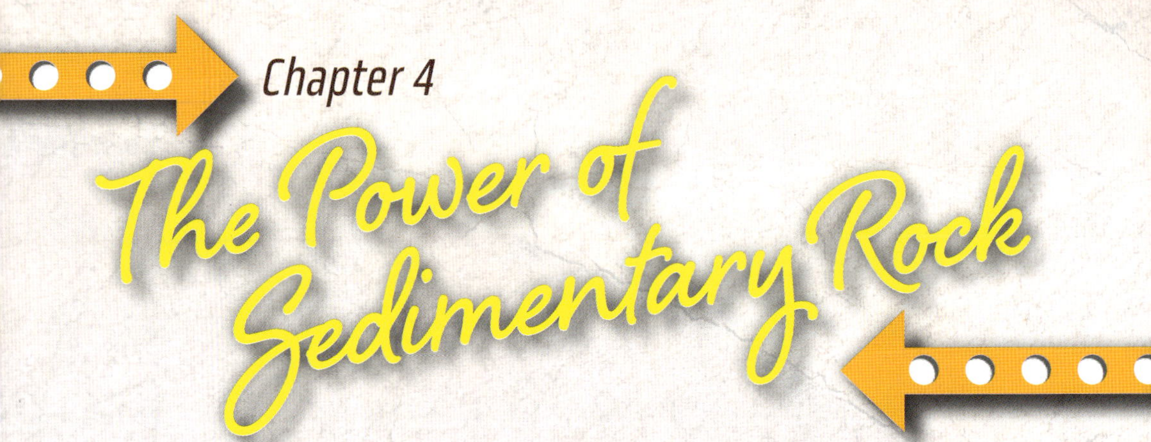

Many people are concerned about the mining of oil in the Alberta oil sands area, which is harming the natural landscape.

Solving Our Energy Issues

Burning fossil fuels releases a gas, called carbon dioxide, into Earth's atmosphere. Carbon dioxide traps heat from the Sun and is causing our planet to become warmer. This global warming is melting ice at the poles and making some places hotter, wetter, drier, or stormier than usual. This is having a huge impact on people, plants, and animals around the world. We are also running out of fossil fuels because they take millions of years to form. People are trying to solve this problem by using more renewable energy, which does not cause global warming and will never run out.

Need for Renewable

Fossil fuels account for almost three-quarters of the emissions created by people in the last 20 years. Scientists are urgently looking for new, cleaner sources of energy so that we can rely less and less on harmful fossil fuels. Renewable energy technologies include wind, water, and solar power.

Digging Deeper

The biggest single oil reserve in the world is the Athabasca oil sands in Alberta, Canada. Oil sands are sediments or sedimentary rocks that are made up of sand, clay minerals, water, and a thick and sticky oil known as bitumen. The Alberta oil sands are unusual because the oil there is found very near to the surface.

A World Without Sedimentary

Imagine life without sedimentary rocks. There would be no coal or oil, no concrete, and no fossils. Sedimentary rocks form much more slowly and less dramatically than igneous rocks, but they are no less important.

Sedimentary rocks are both useful and beautiful.

Always Changing

The shape of our planet's outer surface is constantly changing because of sedimentary rocks. New layers form as sediments are laid down, and old layers weather and erode. This reveals the fossils that the strata contain, which helps us learn more about life on Earth long ago. Many of the most significant events in Earth's history have been dated by looking at sedimentary rock evidence. By studying these rocks, we can find out how animals and plants evolved. We can discover how Earth's climate has changed by studying sedimentary rocks. These rocks provide us with a map of how Earth has been changed and shaped over millions of years.

Rocks Forever?

Sedimentary rocks are useful not only for providing us with fossil fuels and building materials. The grains of sedimentary rocks such as sandstone can also filter dirt from water, which makes it cleaner. We use this freshwater for watering crops, drinking, and for use in factories. Life on Earth would not be the same without sedimentary rock. That is why we must protect Earth and its incredible rock cycle, so sedimentary rock will continue to form for millions of years to come.

Digging Deeper

Sedimentary rocks contain many of the resources that people cannot live without. For example, they hold almost all of Earth's groundwater, which is the water found beneath the surface. This vital water is stored in the spaces and cracks of some of the layers of sedimentary rock. The rocks contain all the world's salt deposits. Sedimentary rocks are also containers for important minerals such as gold and diamonds and the fossil fuels that we are still so reliant on. The rocks truly are a treasure chest of resources.

Sedimentary rocks provide us with important clues about Earth's past.

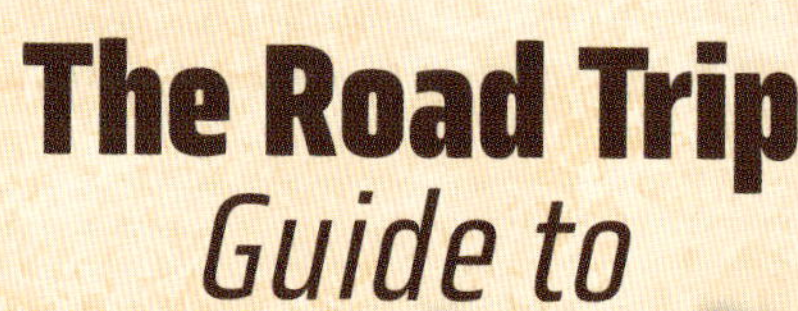

Had a great road trip? Loved the book? Want to try out rock hunting yourself? Awesome! Here's an easy guide that will explain the basics. The great thing about hunting for rocks is that anyone can do it and it costs very little. All you need is a pair of sharp eyes and some resources such as books and websites to help you identify the rocks. A few key pieces of kit help too.

A magnifying glass can help you see the detail in a rock. Try to use a glass that provides five to ten times magnification so you can clearly see the rock.

Keep safe!

Rocks can be sharp, heavy, and hard, and the places where you find them may be dangerous, so it's very important to keep safe. Try to rock hunt in a group and take an adult with you. Rocks can splinter when hit, so always wear goggles when hammering. Tough gloves are useful and a helmet is also important for protection if working near places where rocks could fall.

Hammer and Chisel

The rock hunter's most important tools are a hammer and chisel—and it's worth investing in some proper geological ones. The hammer should mostly be used for splitting stones, and not for breaking stones from cliff faces.

ROCK CLUES

Use these questions to help you identify some of the most common sedimentary rocks.

- Does the rock have fine grains and split into thin, sharp layers? Does it have dull, reddish-brown and fine grains? If you dip an edge of the rock in water and draw it along a white paper surface, does it leave a muddy streak? If the answers are yes, the rock is probably shale.
- Is the rock powdery and easy to break and crumble? Is it white, light gray, or beige? If you pour water onto the rock, does it seep inside a little? If the answers are yes, the rock is probably chalk.
- Is the surface of the rock grainy and rough to touch? When you look very closely at its surface, can you see grains of sand in the rock? When you scratch the surface of the rock, is it difficult to mark? If the answers are yes, the rock is probably limestone.

Geologists always wear safety equipment such as a helmet and goggles when searching for rocks.

How much have you learned about sedimentary rocks and our amazing planet on your road trip? Take the quiz and find out!

1. How is sedimentary rock formed?

2. What causes sedimentary rock to be pressed together?

3. What three layers make up Earth?

4. Where is rock salt formed?

5. Which river system carries more sediment than any other in the world?

6. **What is strata?**

7. **What type of rock can fossils be found in?**

8. **What is the most abundant sedimentary rock on Earth?**

9. **What rock is Table Mountain in South Africa made of?**

10. **Why does chalk easily absorb water?**

ANSWERS

1. By the squeezing together of sediments from other rocks and the remains of living things
2. Pressure from the weight of layers of other rocks above
3. The crust, mantle, and core
4. In dried-up inland seas and salty lakes
5. The Ganges-Brahmaputra river system
6. Layers of sedimentary rock
7. Sedimentary rock
8. Shale
9. Sandstone
10. Because it is porous

GLOSSARY

acids chemical substances that can react with other substances to form salts. Some acids burn or dissolve the substances they come into contact with

aggregate gravel, crushed stone, and sand used to make building materials such as concrete

buttes isolated hills with steep sides and a flat top

calcium carbonate a common substance found in rocks, such as limestone, and which also forms the shells found in nature

canyon a deep gorge that usually has a river running through it, which over time has steadily worn the rock away

coral a hard, stony substance made of calcium carbonate that has formed from the skeletal remains of tiny marine animals

crystals minerals that have a very ordered arrangement of atoms in regular, repeating, symmetrical patterns. When we identify rocks, we call the crystals "grains"

deposits puts or sets down in a particular area or place

desert a barren landscape with little rain or snowfall, making it difficult for plants or animals to survive there

dissolve when a solid mixes with a liquid and becomes part of it, to make a solution

earthquake when the movement of Earth's crust causes a sudden release of energy and the ground shakes at the surface

eruptions violent outbreaks, such as the eruption of molten rock from a volcano

evaporated turned from a liquid into a gas

fertile land or soil that is full of nutrients and good for growing crops

geologists scientists who study Earth and what it is made of

imprints marks or outlines on a surface

impurities substances found in small quantities in another substance, making it less pure

iron oxide a red pigment that gives rocks their red, brownish-red, or pink colors

mined when a substance has been dug or extracted from the ground

minerals substances formed by natural geological processes on Earth. All rocks are made from one or more minerals

nutrients substances that provide nourishment for growth

organic material carbon-based compounds found in nature that come from the remains of living things, such as plants and animals

organic remains the remains of living things such as plants and animals

pressure a continuous physical force exerted on an object by something it is in contact with. Pressure increases underground, for example, because of the downward push of rock above

ravines a deep, narrow gorge with steep sides

resource a supply of something that can be used for a particular purpose

sediment naturally occurring material, such as rocks and the remains of plants and animals, that is broken down by the process of weathering and erosion

species a group of organisms, such as plants or animals, that have similar characteristics and that can breed with one another to produce offspring

UNESCO World Heritage Site a landmark or area that is legally protected by the United Nations because of its cultural, historical, or scientific significance

weathering the wearing away of a substance over time because of the effects of sunlight, wind, water, or other weather conditions

FIND OUT MORE

Books

Fretland VanVoorst, Jennifer. *Sedimentary Rocks* (Rocks and Minerals). Bellwether Media, 2019.

Pettiford, Rebecca. *Sedimentary Rocks* (Geology Genius). Pogo Books, 2018.

Rogers, Marie. *Exploring Sedimentary Rocks* (Let's Rock!). Rosen Publishing Group, 2022.

Websites

Take another look at the rock cycle at:
www.cotf.edu/ete/modules/msese/earthsysflr/rock.html

Test your knowledge about rocks at the DK website:
www.dkfindout.com/uk/earth/rocks-and-minerals

Discover more about sedimentary rocks at:
education.nationalgeographic.org/resource/sedimentary-rock

Learn more about sedimentary rocks at:
kids.britannica.com/kids/article/sedimentary-rock/476316

Publisher's note to educators and parents:
All the websites featured above have been carefully reviewed to ensure that they are suitable for students. However, many websites change often, and we cannot guarantee that a site's future contents will continue to meet our high standards of educational value. Please be advised that students should be closely monitored whenever they access the Internet.

INDEX

ABOUT THE AUTHOR

Sarah Eason has written many books for children on a wide variety of topics, from history to geography and science. She would love to take a rock cycle road trip and visit some of the amazing rocky places explored in this book.